SIZE SEVEN SHORTS

7 SHORT STORIES OF SPIRITUAL INSPIRATION

BY

KATHLEEN MORRIS

Rouge Publishing

Rouge Publishing

978-1-927828-18-2

Other Books By Kathleen Morris

Deep Bay Series
Deep Bay Vengeance
Deep Bay Relic
Deep Bay Legacy (Coming 2014)

Blood War Series
The Prion Attachment
Blood Purge (Coming 2014)

Short Inspirations Series
Size Seven Shorts
Short End Of The Stick
Shortcut To Alaska

Short Stories
Along The Way - 12 Short Stories You Can Read Along
The Way

Plays
Time Will Tell - An Easter Play
Even Me - A Christmas Play For Your Sunday School
All I Need Is Love - A Play For Teens
Lost And Found - A Children's Christmas Play
Gotta Love It - A Humorous Play About Rural Life

How - To Books
How To Make Eye Catching Ebook Covers Easily

Available on Amazon.com

DEDICATION

...for my children

A NOTE FROM THE AUTHOR

Kathleen Morris

Why do I write books?

Simple answer, I can't NOT write books.

For as long as I can remember, I've felt a compulsion to express my creative side. When I was a child, I made up silly little poems and songs and hummed them while skipping to my own beat. In school, I actually hated reading and writing, and I was told I needed to focus more...but I already was, just on my *own* things. Yes, I was a daydreamer, and I still am today.

Throughout my life, as I discovered the wonderful world of words (it took me a while) I began expressing myself through songs and poems of the adult version. I learnt to play guitar but something still didn't feel right. I felt I was meant to do more. Maybe it was that middle kid syndrome growing up that made me feel that way, I don't know. I felt I wasn't important enough because I wasn't the oldest like my big brother. I wasn't even the oldest girl in my family like my big sister. And, I wasn't as important as the youngest, like my little brother. I was just plain old me...*the kid in the middle,* insignificant as I felt. So, the quest my entire life was to matter. I wanted everything I did to matter, what I thought, what I did, what I wrote...and what I write today. Perhaps this is a dysfunction, but whatever you want to label it...*it is me.*

And so I began one of the most profound journeys of my life: My writing career. I didn't do it to make money, yes, that always helps, but it started out my passion and still is. I wrote when my kids were young and became frustrated because I didn't know what exactly I was suppose to do to get my books out there. My first book sat on a shelf collecting dust for ten years.

Now that my kids are grown and on their own, I decided to blow off the dust of my old forgotten novels, and get them published. Little by little, I put one foot forward to seek my dream to become an author...and every day I'm challenged to find the time. I work full time at a busy cable company, and still try to squeeze in as much writing time as possible. I wake up early, two hours before my shift starts every day, and write my heart out. Yes, finding time to write is a constant struggle, but I will do anything to make time for my passion.

I call writing, my passion, because I want other people to learn from my experiences. I have been through a lot of hard things and the only way I have made it, is because of my faith. I am a Christian, and follower of Jesus Christ, my saviour and friend. He has helped me through so many things. I want to share that. I want to write my experiences and show how God has helped me through, in hopes that others may share in the blessing. This is my purpose, my drive, my destiny in life...my reason for writing.

And if this isn't enough reason for writing, I have one more that burns inside my chest. Not only do I want to matter, but I want God's words to matter. I want everything I write to lead people to Christ. Perhaps you can call me an evangelist, I don't know. But what I do know is that I am a non-traditionalist. I don't evangelize in the normal way, I do it through my characters. Yes, I also write true stories about my own life, and love to encourage and help others through difficulties as God helped me, but I have an imagination too. I like to create flawed characters and watch them learn and grow into the men and woman God intended them to be.

I don't write about perfect people, or make it seem like Christian's have it all together because we don't. I don't! I'm flawed, just like the next person. I make mistakes like everyone else. The only difference is I'm saved by God's grace and he helps me through the tough times. I want my characters to do the same so that my reader fans can relate to them and learn through them...and ultimately turn to Jesus for a love so unbelievable, it makes your heart sing. And...I want my readers to know...they are loved no matter what, no matter how screwed up and flawed they are...because he loves us ALL!

Why do I write books?

Because I matter to me, and I matter to God...*and so do you!*

TABLE OF CONTENTS

HOW TO MAKE LEMONADE

When life gives you lemons is it easy to make lemonade?

I've been thinking of this question since I became a victim of armed robbery at work in May. I wasn't the one directly facing the robber but the one hidden at my desk. One might think that would be the better place to be, but seeing everything unfolding in front of me made my life flash before my eyes and that has haunted me ever since.

Yes I am getting over it, and for the most part I faired well compared to the countless others who have been injured or killed in similar situations. However, it doesn't serve as any comfort at all because a threat to your life is real no matter whether it comes from Arnold Schwarzenegger or Tiny Tim.

Fear has become my lemon in such a way that it has soured my once safe environment and left me trying to rid myself of the foul aftertaste that seems to linger where I least expect it.

So…my question is how do I make lemonade out of this?

I'm usually a person who bounces back quite easily and tries to make the best of every situation. But this is different. This isn't your normal hardship. And maybe I don't even know what real hardship is…but that doesn't mean I can't recognize the simple fact that to make lemonade one must squeeze.

As I thought about this, my squeezing actually began before I even realized I was doing it. It was hindsight that clearly brought it to mind that first day when I thought I was okay but kept on shaking. It began when I got home and cried for two days. It began when I talked with the trauma councillor my first day back to work when I had to physically walk back into the office. It began when I allowed myself to morn the loss of my power that had been taken from me.

It's only when we peel the skin off a lemon that we really begin the work we need to do. I had to let myself feel. You see, many people block their emotions because it hurts, but that just makes it harder to process the juice of the situation. You really need the peelings off before you even start.

Little by little as I processed what was needed, I realized I had so much misplaced fear I needed to put it back in its place. Every now and then especially dealing with confrontational customers again at work, I started shaking with that same panic and fear from the robbery. It seemed to rear its ugly head in situations where it didn't belong and I needed to do something about it before it got any worse.

Like pulp and seeds in a crystal clear juice, I had to remove that spoiling agent. The question was how? Well, I'd like to say I came up with it all by myself, but I didn't. It was through my trauma councillor that I became aware of the proper procedure in which to do this. Firstly, I had to get my stolen power back. I had to stand up for myself, and that has always been hard for me at the best of times leave alone the worst.

After reclaiming victory over my life in certain situations and being proactive in dealing with miserable customers, I slowly began to assert myself. I remember the first time I was successful in this at work. I had a customer I asked to step back from my side of the counter, I had another I told

I wouldn't help if she didn't talk to me in a respectful manner. It was a changing experience and one that gave me power in an otherwise powerless situation…and power is what is absolutely necessary when changing ones circumstances.

Once you peel the lemons and you start to squeeze you know the only way to get the lemonade you so greatly desire is with some sort of power. A weak arm won't do it; I know that much. Weakness is a hindrance for anyone who has gone through any kind of pain or trauma much worse than I have. It can leave a person so powerless and hopeless that depression sets in and holds you in bondage to fear for the rest of your life.

So, be powerful!

Joshua 1:9 says, "*Have I not commanded you? Be strong and courageous. Do not be terrified; do not be discouraged, for the LORD your God will be with you wherever you go.*"

These words make me jump for joy because it is through this verse that I understand the need for Christ in my life. He is my special ingredient which drives my life force, empowering me to press on and strive toward the goal.

So, going back to my original question… 'When life gives you lemons is it easy to make lemonade?' I say absolutely no! Of course it isn't easy to make lemonade, but it is possible with the proper process and ingredients.

Like any good drink a sweetener is always required. I know without the sweetness of God in my life I would have been a bitter old woman long ago. I rejoice in the fact that we can overcome obstacles and hardships and make that lemonade if we want to, but unfortunately many people don't understand how to make it, and some don't even think to make it their drink of choice at all.

I'm glad I have an acquired taste!

GREAT BIG PUDDLE OF PEE

My kids were bullied in School.

It was a harsh reality, but something they faced every day growing up in rural Saskatchewan. I don't know why they were targeted but perhaps it was because we were the new people who hadn't grown up there.

Many years have gone by since that time but I still remember the tears, bloody noses, and hardships my children faced, and my many attempts to protect them. Naturally, as a mom I wanted to ensure they had a place to play where they felt loved, so one winter I set out to do just that.

Even though the town ice rink was only a couple miles down the road, I decided to make a bully-free ice rink on our own farm. It was supposed to be a place they could skate without ridicule or harassment.

Without much experience, I set out to prepare the ground for the rink. The kids and I decided upon a spot right in front of the kitchen window that proved to be the flattest.

As my kids counted out the exact steps for a perfect square, I smiled at the beginnings of a primitive ice rink where they could play without being picked on. It was a wonderful feeling as if I were punishing the town for being so cruel. I wanted to shout, "Take that you bullies! You can't get my kids here!"

Soon we started filling buckets with hot water and lumbering them out to the rink-site one by one, slowly saturating the frosty steaming ground. I didn't really know if I was supposed to use hot water or cold but I heard somewhere that hot water made the best rink, so we continued until the hot water tank died. After that, we started using cold water.

Finally after spending our entire Christmas holidays hauling buckets out to the rink, we declared it finished on New Years Eve. We laced up our skates, cranked up the music, and pranced across the bumpy uneven surface under the stars. It wasn't perfect with its bubbles and holes, but it was our private oasis that nobody could see but us.

The first day of school in January brought on a panic I hadn't expected. The school bus had to pick up the kids in front of the house, and that meant the bullies would see the ice rink. At first I hadn't worried too much about it. The kids were proud of their creation not ashamed.

When the bus rolled into the yard and stopped in front of the ice rink, every child on it pasted their evil faces against the cold foggy windows, looking at the ice rink, laughing hysterically. My heart broke as I watched my little happy angels drop their heads in shame.

I wondered why they thought it was funny. Sure it was lumpy, uneven, and probably not a perfect square, but that shouldn't matter to a bunch of kids.

When they returned home, the bus dropped the kids off again and the same thing happened all over again. This time my kids ran into the house with hot steamy tears rolling down their cherub faces.

"They said it's a pee rink!" my oldest shouted through sobs as she tore off her jacket and headed to her room.

Why would they say such a thing?

After much consoling, I found out the reason. The one thing we had not considered while making this rink was our water. It came from a rusty old well and it was orange. So, naturally the rink looked like it was a pee yellow.

My heart sank! "Lord," I cried. "No matter what we do, they still find a way to pick on my kids!"

It was only after many years that I began to realize the lesson in it all. God didn't want us to hide from the bullies. He didn't want me to teach my kids to run from trouble. He wanted me to teach them to face their fears and rely on Jesus Christ to save them instead of me.

Today, my kids are pretty resilient. Without the bullies, they wouldn't be the people they are today. God was molding and making them bit by bit just like our imperfect ice rink. And when we face rejection because of the way we look, live, or act, stay strong because God loves us flaws and all!

Even if we're pee yellow!

FOOTSTEPS IN THE SNOW

Have you ever noticed how different we all are?

I went to the gym the other day and walked on the treadmill. Usually I find it pretty boring because there isn't much to do during this activity, so I invented my own. Actually I didn't do it on purpose; there wasn't anywhere else for me to stare.

Three other people in front of me were walking the treadmill, so I watched them. (I know, creepy!) But while I was watching, I noticed how each one had a slightly different stride. Some waddled like an ape, some lumbered, and some walked without swaying side to side at all.

My own gate is pretty motionless. I don't swing my hips around at all like most women. In fact, I pretty much walk like a man. Funny, I know, but that is me.

As I was watching the treadmill people, my mind drifted back to when I was a kid. I use to walk to school with my big sister and I had to make a point of deliberately slowing or speeding my stride so I would not match hers. I use to hate the crunch, crunch, crunch in the snow as we walked in unison together.

I wanted to be me. I was not my sister, nor did I want to be like her. Nothing was wrong with her; in fact she is a beautiful person inside and out. I just wanted to be different.

I think of how different we are as Christians as we worship, sing, learn, and live individually. God obviously made us all unique for a reason, so that made me realize we should embrace that fact.

It's just so easy to pick at other believers because they don't raise their hands when they worship, or close their eyes. We judge others because they don't dress up Sunday mornings or they stand outside the church puffing on their cigarettes before taking a seat in the sanctuary.

If we were all the same, wouldn't that be boring?

Then I started to wonder why God made us so strangely different. What did he possibly want us to learn from this?

Acceptance perhaps? If I started accepting other people and their different ways, wouldn't that make me love more?

Maybe love was the point all along?!

If God can love us for all our silly quirks shouldn't we love others? 1 John 4:11 says, "Dear Friends, since God so loved us, we also ought to love on another." (NIV)

So whether we walk like an ape or raise our hands to pray, or if we think our differences or others differences are strange, remember that God loves us just the way we are and we should do the same!

REFUGE

Have you ever caught yourself thinking life is too hard?

I have many a time. In fact, I find the winter months are the worst for me. Not only is it cold, but it's dark and depressing as well. This year winter dragged on far too long and March was filled with a month of loathing…waiting…sickness…and impatience. If there ever was a month to brand as troublemaker, it was March sticking up its hand saying, "Pick me! Pick me!"

I wonder why the weather impacts our emotions so much?

No matter what month it is, storms in particular seem to set certain moods. Rain for instance gives me an overwhelming feeling that it is time to put everything into perspective. I don't know why. Maybe that's just me and everyone else has a little different take on it.

Violent rainstorms bring out the worst in me. I am a big chicken and am very afraid. Others chase tornados and get a thrill from it.

Regardless of how vastly different our emotions are and how they are individually triggered by the weather, one thing remains constant: We all go through the storms one way or the other.

I think back to the biggest storm in my life. We were in the process of moving our young family to a small town on a hot day in July. Throughout the moving process, the humidity was rising and the deep dark clouds built on the horizon.

It wasn't enough to be moving that day, but we had decided to move into our garage because the mobile home we had purchased needed sever renovations. So, after a long day of labour, we set up beds for the kids and ourselves, a makeshift kitchen on one side and a shabby couch on the other for a living room. A large orange tarp divided our sleeping quarters from the rest of the garage.

What were we thinking?!

Finally, after blood sweat and tears, we were ready to call it a night and headed to our church to clean up because we didn't have washing facilities set up. (Yeah, I'm shaking my head too.) Anyway, as we headed for the truck, we noticed the black and green sky above as the wind started to pick up dramatically.

It was a tornado!

Quickly we headed for the church as the power went out. Once inside the enormous gymnasium-type structure, we rummaged around for a safe place to wait out the storm. It was the baptismal tank we ultimately decided upon in the midst of sheer terror.

All I can remember was the horrifying freight-train sound that whooshed around the building for hours. I could barely hear the Sunday school songs I was singing to the kids to calm them down. Stranger's kids had joined us in the baptismal tank after stopping at the church to take refuge as well, and that made for a lot of shivering, sobbing children to sooth.

I absolutely thought those three hours huddled in the baptismal tank would never end.

Finally around midnight, we ventured out to check what was left of our town. It wasn't good. Roofs were ripped off houses, shingles, fences, and trees littered the streets like never before. It was a miracle we had made it through.

When we got back to our garage/home, we were devastated that all our hard work of setting up the garage was for nothing. The windows had broken in the storm and everything was sopped. Yes, it could have been worse but we still had a home. Our mobile just had water damage but we actually had hoped it would have blown away so we didn't have to do our renovations. But it sustained the effects of the storm just fine because it was the oldest, heaviest beast on the block. All we could do was laugh.

Blessings come in mysterious ways, and after a storm you have to be pretty creative to actually see them.

It took us a long time to fix and renovate our mobile home and garage that year. Six months to be exact. It was a hard six months living in our garage and showering at truck stops with our kids, but we did it.

I shake my head along with everyone else reading this. How did we do it? Why did we do it? We could have given up when the storm hit. We could have walked away from the renovations…but we didn't. We persevered.

It was just one of many storms in my life...and now I know, it was God who gave me the strength to get through!

Life IS hard! It's hard all the time! Everyone has their challenges. Everyone has their storms. In fact, right at this moment as some of you read this…a battle may be brewing in your own life. Maybe there is a storm you are facing and you need a safe place to wait it out. I encourage you to seek the only safe place available…Jesus Christ!

He can be your safe place, your refuge! *Take comfort in a favourite Bible verse that has gotten me through many a storm: "God is our refuge and strength, an ever-present help in trouble. Therefore we will not fear, though the earth give way and the mountains fall into the heart of the sea, though its waters roar and foam and the mountains quake with their surging."* Psalm 46:1-3 (NIV).

So, hold on tight when the storms of life come along. Don't let those awful winters or endless Marches discourage you. Don't give up when life is too hard!

Keep going until you see the light shine again!

I leave you with a poem I wrote years ago that was published in a book anthology. It pretty well sums it up.

Refuge

When the clouds of heaven look like you feel,

And you can no longer hold back the tears;

When life never seems to work out at all,

And you've had problems for so many years;

When the end looks far and the tunnel is long,

And the light has all but gone out;

When you don't know why you even bother sometimes,

And your head is consumed with doubt;

Forget the world and all that it is,

And run to the safest place,

A place of peace, and joy, and love,

A place of saving grace.

And there you'll find a special friend,

He'll teach you how to pray.

He is the God of refuge and strength:

Jesus will love you today!

Thank you for reading and I hope I brightened your day and gave you the encouragement you were seeking.

BRINGING HOME THE COWS

It was a foggy morning when I answered the door wondering who was rapping so early. Our farm was situated amongst a group of others so it wasn't usual to have a neighbour drop by. Still, there was nothing normal about this visit.

"Your cow's are out," I was told.

We had two calves, a heifer, and a bull calf but they were more like the kid's pets than livestock. It was our first attempt at ranching if you could even call it that. Little did we know we actually had to feed them more than grass in the middle of October. They were starving and hopped the fence for greener pasture.

The kids called our cows Jack and Jill, and as the old nursery rhyme goes, they both had a pretty bad tumble. Our real life Jack and Jill were no exception. Jill had been hit on the side of the highway by a transport and Jack was apparently standing by her side. So off we went to rescue them in our old car. Since my husband needed my help, I had to go along as well as the kids because they were just pre-schoolers and couldn't stay alone.

Creeping along the highway, my husband and I kept our eyes peeled for Jack and Jill. It was hard to see because of the fog but we pushed on anyway. The kids were oblivious to the calamity; they just thought we were going on an adventure trip. I just kept praying for a happy ending.

Suddenly we spotted a bull calf on the side of the foggy highway and pulled over. It was Jack standing a few feet away from Jill. She was still alive but obviously suffering. "Stay here with the kids!" my husband ordered as he got out. He opened the trunk and readied a shotgun.

I was not prepared for that! Immediately I jumped out of the vehicle, questioning him and reminding him that Jack and Jill were the kid's pets and he could not put an animal down in front of them no matter how bad it was suffering. So, we decided the best thing to do was for me to take the kids to the nearest town and fill up the car with gas, and I was to leave my lunatic husband standing on the side of the highway with a shotgun. All the way to town I prayed, hoping my babies did not understand. The oldest had just turned five so I didn't really know.

By the time I was done filling up the car, giving my husband ample time to do the awful deed; I was able to catch my breath. I prayed for direction in how to tell the kids, and surrendered the whole thing to him. I was ready to head back to get my husband, or so I thought.

With the fog still causing zero visibility, I found myself proceeding down the highway at a snails pace until I finally came to a stop. It was a roadblock! Panic consumed me. Every thought imaginable entered my head. Did my husband accidentally shoot someone? Did he shoot himself? Finally, a police officer approached my vehicle and told me a passer by had called in a report that a man with a shotgun had his family hold up along side the highway.

My face fell a thousand shades of red.

I gulped through the tears and embarrassment, trying to explain what was going on and that I needed to get through the roadblock. Reluctantly, the officer agreed to let me go and I advanced through the eerie fog like a scene from Star Trek. With zero visibility we crept the desolate highway with no definite direction. The kids were still and quiet in their car seats as I steadied my shaking hands on the steering wheel. "Lord! I prayed. "Help us!"

Without warning, two ghostly figures appeared in front of me causing me to jolt my car to a sudden stop. It was non other than my crazy spouse and a female police officer trying to lasso a very ticked off bull calf.

As the story goes, we got through the roadblock safely to the other side despite the obstacles in our way. Jack was eventually dragged home and no charges were laid. The kids were told that Jill had died and they also learned to survive the shock as I did, to find out we actually had to eat her for future dinners. Needless to say, none of us had much of an appetite after that.

Yes, that was quite the story. One I tell often. But no story is without its lessons and there were many to be found with this one. Besides the obvious like don't carry a loaded shotgun along side the highway, there is a spiritual lesson as well. I know that we are not cows but lets think for a minute in that general direction. Don't we do the same things that cows do sometimes? When we don't get what we want, we often run for greener pastures and usually end up getting ourselves into trouble like Jack and Jill did. We fumble around in the fog trying to find our way back home only to realize we are hopelessly lost.

Well, all is not lost!

God wants the prodigal to come home. Luke 15:5-7 says, *"Rejoice with me; I have found my lost sheep. I tell you that in the same way there will be more rejoicing in heaven over one sinner who repents than over ninety-nine righteous persons who do not need to repent."* (NIV). Whether it is sheep, cows, your troubled teenager, or yourself who is lost, God rejoices when you come home. He wants to find you and save you from a life of sin and suffering so that you don't end up as road kill along side a highway of regret.

So...Why not come out of the fog?!!

THE SPECIALIST

Insecurities are something we all struggle with, especially me!

The other day I went jean shopping for the first time in a long time and it was quite the ordeal. Normally I buy jeans from a second hand shop but this time I was told not to be so cheap and spend my money on a new pair.

So, off I went shopping with my sister who had a dickens of a time trying to convince me to make up my mind. Really, I was in tears trying to find something that wasn't made for teenagers or twenty somethings. Low rise jeans just didn't fit someone my age.

Finally, I had to resort to asking a jeanologist to help. Yes, I didn't even know they existed. She was apparently a specialist who lead me to the perfect fitting jeans tailor made for a woman my age.

I was very thankful for my jeanologist that day, and wonder how often we think of God in that way. Do we fumble through problems without the guidance we need, trying to handle everything ourselves, or do we ask for advice?

We don't have to wait until we are at our wits end or crying our eyes out before we ask for help. God wants us to call on Him daily! Matthew 7:7 says, "*Ask, and it shall be given you; seek, and ye shall find; knock, and it shall be opened unto you.*" (KJV) So, when you're facing difficult times, or you simply don't know how to do something, call on our Saviour Jesus Christ.

Why? Because He's the specialist!

HONEY PAIL LOVE

Ah yes, I was young, naïve, and absolutely out of my mind agreeing to buy such a ridiculous house. At that point in my life, I didn't need a lot of convincing. Whenever my husband wanted something, all he had to do was grin at me and I would melt.

"I love it honey," I smiled at him, fluttering my eyelashes like some star struck teenager, even though the house was a throwback to the pioneer era.

With two toddlers in tow, and a baby in my arms, we moved in to our prehistoric dive with visions of grandeur. "I'll fix it up babe," he beamed like the hunky stud that he was. Of course, like a fool I fell for it, dreaming right along with him.

It didn't take me long to realize we had made a terrible mistake, but instead of complaining about it, I decided to tough it out like a good little wife should. I scrubbed the dirty walls, I swept the painted wooden floors, and I even put up some fancy yellow curtains in the kitchen to prove our funny home was just fine.

Tight quarters started bothering me, but the kids didn't seem to mind. They shared a bedroom, playing every evening when they were supposed to be sleeping. We'd get mad at them, but really, it wasn't their fault. We had to stuff their toy box in the same room with them because it wouldn't fit anywhere else.

Laundry was a chore. I was one of those mothers that thought cloth diapers were the way to go. WRONG! It was exhausting. Most of time the water heater didn't work and neither did the dryer –so I hung the wash outside. I guess I thought, "Why not ACT like a pioneer woman," I certainly FELT like one. At least I didn't have to use a washboard though the washer was a close second with its Mickey Mouse plumbing.

The plumbing issue bothered me the most. THERE WAS NO PLUMBING! When I first discovered this, I darted from one room to another, hoping it wasn't true. Black pipe stuck through the wall to the outside from the kitchen sink, the washing machine, and yes, the bathroom.

They call it a "honey pail." It's a metal can with a bucket inside. That was our toilet. One of my chores was to empty the rancid thing. I'd have to daily lift an overly filled plastic pail and haul it all the way to the backyard outhouse. Try to do that without a splash, it's just impossible.

"I can't raise my babies here!" I yelled at my husband one day after I couldn't stand it anymore. He tried to comfort me and told me about his numerous renovation plans. They sounded so wonderful, but I didn't think I could wait any longer for him to fix the house. He had to do something or I was going to leave.

I spent every night on my knees, praying for strength to persevere. I wanted to obey my husband, but I was weary.

Winter hit with a vengeance, and it was bitterly cold in that poorly insulated shack. Plumbing pipes that emptied outside froze up, leaving a bathtub of dirty water that wouldn't empty and no way to wash the diapers, or the kids. Dishwater wouldn't drain, and dirty dishes piled everywhere. I boiled water and took the kettle outside to pour the hot water over the frozen drainpipes. That's when it all changed.

My husband came home from work early one day and caught me in tears, shivering in the cold as I hammered away on the frozen bathtub drainpipe outside while the kids bawled inside at the window. I was at my wits end. I screamed a prayer for God to get us out of there.

It turned out that my husband was home early because he lost his job. It was a blessing in disguise and an answer to my prayers. We had to sell and wondered who would buy a place like that. But God is good; he brought someone to buy it right away, someone who actually had the money to fix it up.

One thing I can say about this adventure is that there are no mistakes with God, only lessons: This one was a valuable one for any love-struck woman. I wish I could say that I'll never be that stupid again, but who am I kidding, love is blind.

The End

A NOTE FROM THE AUTHOR

Thank you for reading my true inspirational stories. I hope they touched your heart and made your day brighter. If you would like to read more stories like these, book two called *Short End Of The Stick* in my *Short Inspirations* series is available now at Amazon.com

Other Books By Kathleen Morris

Deep Bay Series
Deep Bay Vengeance
Deep Bay Relic
Deep Bay Legacy (Coming 2014)

Blood War Series
The Prion Attachment
Blood Purge (Coming 2014)

Short Inspirations Series
Size Seven Shorts
Short End Of The Stick
Shortcut To Alaska

Short Stories
Along The Way - 12 Short Stories You Can Read Along
The Way

Plays
Time Will Tell - An Easter Play
Even Me - A Christmas Play For Your Sunday School
All I Need Is Love - A Play For Teens
Lost And Found - A Children's Christmas Play
Gotta Love It - A Humorous Play About Rural Life

How - To Books
How To Make Eye Catching Ebook Covers Easily

Available on Amazon.com